THE INSIDE - OUT STOMACH
An Introduction to Animals without Backbones

THE INSIDE - OUT STOMACH
An Introduction to Animals without Backbones

by Peter Loewer
illustrated by Jean Jenkins

ATHENEUM   1990   NEW YORK

Collier Macmillan Canada
TORONTO

Maxwell Macmillan International Publishing Group
NEW YORK   OXFORD   SINGAPORE   SYDNEY

Dedicated to *The Sea for Sam*,
hours spent at the shores of pools and ponds,
Dr. W. D. Russell-Hunter,
and young nieces and nephews everywhere

Atheneum
Macmillan Publishing Company
866 Third Avenue
New York, NY 10022

Collier Macmillan Canada, Inc.
1200 Eglinton Avenue East
Suite 200
Don Mills, Ontario M3C 3N1

First Edition
Printed in the United States of America
1 2 3 4 5 6 7 8 9 10

Library of Congress Cataloging-in-Publication Data
Loewer, H. Peter.
The inside-out stomach: an introduction to animals without
backbones/by Peter Loewer; illustrated by Jean Jenkins.—1st ed.
p.   cm.
Bibliography: p.
Includes index.
Summary: Describes the physical characteristics, habits, and
natural environment of a variety of animals that do not have a
backbone. Includes amoebas and other one-celled animals, worms,
insects, lobsters, and others.
ISBN 0-689-31432-9
1. Invertebrates—Juvenile literature. [1. Invertebrates.]
I. Jenkins, Jean, ill. II. Title.
QL362.L64 1990
592—dc19   89-6499   CIP   AC

CONTENTS

INTRODUCTION

Over one million different kinds, or species, of animals share space on our planet earth.

   With your two eyes, two legs, backbone that bends, and thumb that moves in all directions, you are a human being and a mammal. An animal with fins and a body covered with scales, which breathes underwater, is a fish. A centipede with its one hundred legs, hard, shell-like body, and no backbone is called an arthropod. Each is a different physical type and each has its own name.

Keeping Track of a Million Different Animals

Zoologists, who study animals, created two imaginary file cabinets, each with many drawers. Each drawer in these cabinets is called a *phylum* (pronounced fi'lum). Each one contains many animals that are similar. The first cabinet is full of animals that have backbones. The second cabinet is full of animals that are able to live perfectly well without them.

Animals with Backbones

An animal with a backbone is called a vertebrate (pronounced ver'ta-brate). A backbone is made of individual pieces called *vertebrae* (pronounced ver'ta-bray). The vertebrae are all connected like beads on a string. The string is flexible and can bend, twist, and turn.

The backbone holds your head and neck up, and it also holds up your rib cage and joins your *pelvis* to your legs.

Your dog or cat has a backbone and a skeleton that looks much like yours—only smaller. And believe it or not, even the snake's skeleton resembles your skeleton. But its arms and legs have become very small so they can fit within its long, narrow skin.

Yet one of the most amazing things about backbones is the number of animals that don't have them.

A boy and his dog, both vertebrates, imagine they meet an octopus, an animal without a backbone.

BACKBONE

BACKBONE

Animals without Backbones

Many animals on earth are still able to move about and live their lives without the help of this support. They can live without a backbone because:

1. they float in the ocean and in ponds, like the jellyfish, and the water supports their fragile bodies;

2. they live inside a hard shell, like the snail, and this gives them all the protection they need;

3. they have a tough outer skin, like the garden slug and the earthworm, and during the day live under rocks or deep in the soil to protect themselves from the hot sun; or

4. they have a tough outer body that moves like armor, following their every movement. This group includes crabs, crayfish, and beetles.

There are about thirty times as many animals that do not have a backbone as animals that do have them. These animals are called *invertebrates*. Invertebrate is a scientific term that means "without a backbone," or without vertebrae. These animals, from the one-celled amoeba (pronounced a-me′ba) to the starfish with the inside-out stomach, are the subject of this book.

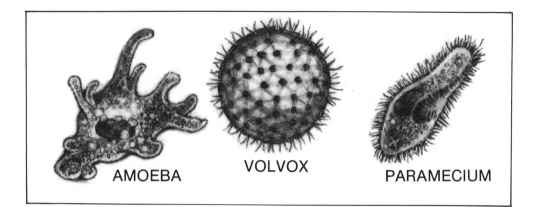

AMOEBA VOLVOX PARAMECIUM

PROTOZOANS: The One-Celled Animals

The slow-moving *amoeba*, the fast *paramecium*, and the whirling *volvox* are all one-celled animals and belong to the phylum called *Protozoa*. Every human body has billions of cells and each protozoan has only one, yet protozoans can still do many of the same things humans can do. They can eat, travel, and even create new protozoans.

The word *protozoa* means first animal. Most scientists believe that these were the first forms of animal life on earth. *Fossils* of Protozoa have been found that are over 1.5 billion years old. Most biologists believe that there are more than 100,000 different species of Protozoa in the world today, still waiting to be discovered.

Protozoans either live separately, like the amoeba, or in colonies of many individuals, like the volvox. A volvox makes itself into a round ball of many identical one-celled animals. By living together, each individual volvox helps the others in finding food, and the colony can move faster through the water than a single volvox could.

If you fill a jar with water from a pond and include some water weeds and rocks and soil from the bottom, you will have a miniature water world full of thousands of protozoans, many of them visible as tiny dots moving through the water. But not all of the animals in the jar are Protozoa. Some of them are other members of the animal world, like tiny worms and small insects.

Although a *microscope* is a handy tool, even a hand lens will enable you to see many of the single-celled pond inhabitants. The drawing illustrates a few of the many one-celled animals found in clean pond water.

One of the most interesting protozoans is the amoeba. There are many different species of amoeba. Some live in ponds, some in salt water, some are found in damp soil, and a few live as parasites in the digestive tracts of animals. When people travel from country to country and are not careful to drink only clean water, they may become infected with an intestinal disease caused by a species of amoeba.

The pond amoeba is probably the most common species of amoeba in the world. It lives in unpolluted water, on the surface of submerged leaves or on the dirt or silt at the bottom of a pond. A typical one is about the size of a small pinhead. Even under a microscope, an amoeba is easy to miss because it is transparent and moves very, very slowly.

Most of an amoeba's cell is made of a liquid called *cytoplasm.* This liquid is held in by a cell membrane, a tough material that acts as the animal's skin. Under the microscope, the central mass of cytoplasm is seen as a fluid full of material that looks like tiny grains of sand. This is bounded by a clear, outer jellylike layer.

Floating in the midst of the central grainy cytoplasm is a round mass of very dense material that is the *nucleus* of the cell

PSEUDOPODS
An amoeba moves with its pseudopods.

6

and acts like a brain for the animal. If an amoeba is divided so that one half contains the nucleus and the other half does not, the part with the nucleus will continue to grow while the other half will die.

Amoebas both move and eat by flowing into extensions of their bodies called *pseudopods* (pronounced su'do-pods), a scientific word that means false feet. If all its pseudopods were pulled back into its body, the amoeba would be round.

When it wishes to move, the amoeba sends out a pseudopod that looks like one of the fingers on a rubber glove. Soon the cell contents flow into it. As the pseudopod becomes larger, the amoeba sends out other fingers from it in the direction it wants to go. The cell contents flow into these new fingers, which in turn send out more fingers. This is the way the animal travels.

If an amoeba finds something to eat, like a smaller protozoan or a piece of miniature plant life called alga, it sends out a number of pseudopods to surround the food. Then the food is enclosed in a small bit of the amoeba's skin—like a tiny balloon—with the food inside. There it is digested and absorbed directly into the body. The amoeba has no mouth.

An amoeba also takes in a lot of water through the cell membrane, and after a time it could become so full of water it could burst. But the amoeba has a bubblelike organ floating in the cytoplasm that acts like a small pump, and when water builds up in the amoeba's body, this pump fills up with the extra water and releases it to the outside through a small opening in the cell membrane.

An amoeba breathes by taking oxygen directly from the surrounding water through other very tiny openings in the cell membrane.

The amoeba reproduces by simply dividing its nucleus and then itself into two parts.

NUCLEUS

An amoeba surrounds a smaller protozoa with its pseudopods.

CYTOPLASM

GLASS SPONGE

BATH SPONGE

FRESHWATER SPONGE

PORIFERA: Animals Full of Holes

What animal has no heart, no lungs, no brain or nervous system, and, except when it's very young, never moves from one place to another for its entire life? The answer is the sponge.

For hundreds of years, biologists thought that sponges were undersea plants because all they did was grow larger with the passage of time. Then, in the nineteenth century, it was discovered that they were animals, related to Protozoa.

The phylum *Porifera* (pronounced por-i-fer′a) represents about five thousand species of sponges. The word *porifera* means full of holes. Although they seem to be the most boring of creatures, sponges make up for any lack of action with their fantastic variety of forms and their beautiful colors. Recently, a number of saltwater sponges have been found to be able to resist infection, and scientists hope to be able to develop new medicines by studying them.

Although most sponges come from the ocean, a few are found in fresh water. Freshwater sponges often grow on stones or submerged pieces of wood in slow-moving streams. They look like flat patches of a brownish green crust, often with fingerlike projections. Those sponges found in ponds are usually even smaller and attach themselves to submerged plant stems.

Sponges have been gathered from the sea for thousands of years. The ancient Romans used them as paintbrushes and mops, and not too long ago, everyone used sponges for bathing in the tub and for doing dishes at the kitchen sink. Centuries ago, divers held their breath while they looked for sponges on the sea bottom, but later, men wore complicated diving suits that enabled them to gather more of these valuable creatures. Today most divers wear simpler scuba tanks, but in any case, most sponges we use in the home are man-made.

Sponges may be as small as one half inch in width or as large as forty inches wide. A few are over six feet high. But, large or small, each sponge is a creature made of hundreds of thousands of one-celled animals all living together in a way that offers shelter and protection for each member of the group.

A good way to describe this is to compare it to a large underwater apartment building where water comes in via the windows, travels through many smaller rooms and hallways, and finally leaves through the chimney at the top. This current of water brings food and carries oxygen to the individual cells and carries away their carbon dioxide and other animal wastes.

Some sponge cells produce *spicules*. These are pieces of a tough material that helps hold the softer parts of the creature together. Spicules are made either of glasslike *silica* or other mineral crystals, or, in the bath sponge, a soft protein called *spongin*.

Special cells line all rooms and hallways inside the sponge. Each of these cells has one long whip that it continually waves about. The combined action of thousands of these whips moves the water along the sponge passageways and brings small bits of food in from the outside. The whips pull food particles within reach of other special cells where they are digested. Another kind of cell, called an *amoebocyte* (pronounced a-me'bo-cite and named after its resemblance to an amoeba), is able to move around within the body of the sponge and distribute the digested food to the other cells.

Biologists have looked for years to find out if sponges have any nervous system that could send messages of pain or hunger to the various cells, but so far there doesn't seem to be one. Unlike more active animals, each of the cells in a sponge goes on about its business in its own way, with little or no cooperation from the others. But if sponge tissue is forced through a fine silk cloth and all the cells are completely jumbled up, they will soon reassemble themselves and form a new animal.

All sponges reproduce sexually by producing female eggs and male *sperm*—often both come from the same animal—that unite to form a small single cell. This cell divides and grows and soon becomes a group of cells with waving whips that force it through the water. When it finds a spot of its own, it settles down and grows larger. And it never moves again.

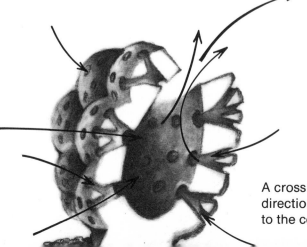

A cross section of a living sponge. The arrows show the direction of the water as it's pulled through openings to the center of the animal.

TENTACLE

TRIGGER

STINGING
CELLS

An enlarged
view of a
jellyfish tentacle.

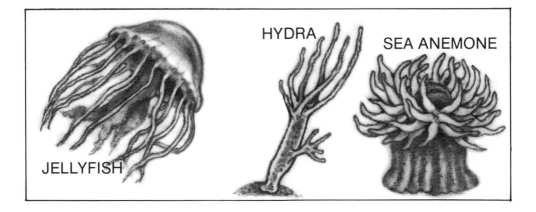

JELLYFISH

HYDRA

SEA ANEMONE

CNIDARIA: Stingers of Ponds and Oceans

Every summer, along the seacoasts of America, there are warnings of jellyfish invasions. Not only are you told to avoid jellyfish while swimming in the open sea, you are also advised not to step on them if they wash ashore onto the beach. Even when they are dead, parts of these animals will react automatically to the pressure of your foot and sting enough to cause a great deal of pain.

How can such a harmless-looking animal, an animal made of a blob of glistening jelly, be harmful?

The answer is that jellyfish have stinging capsules that are used both for protection from enemies—including you—and for gathering food. Jellyfish, sea anemones, corals, and the freshwater hydras are some of the almost eleven thousand species belonging to the phylum *Cnidaria* (pronounced ni-da′ri-a). All look harmless enough, but all are successful hunters because they have stinging capsules, or cells.

These capsules are a cunning invention of nature. Although they are very small and only visible under a microscope, these stinging machines can inflict a painful wound. One capsule may not be noticed, but thousands of them stinging at the same time can paralyze a victim. The stingers of small hydras are not strong enough to penetrate the human skin, but those of the larger jellyfish can be very dangerous.

The tentacles of these animals, which look like very thin threads waving about in the water, bear thousands of stinging cells. Each one looks like a bottle with a rounded bottom and an extremely long, narrow, hollow neck that is coiled around it. Each bottle also has a tiny trigger that projects into the water. When that trigger is touched, the neck of the bottle uncoils at lightning speed and shoots out into the victim, where it releases a dose of poison. The beauty of the system is that the larger the victim, the more triggers it touches and the more poison it receives by injection.

You need not visit the ocean to see an animal that uses these stinging cells. Three species of hydras are often found living on plants growing in pond water: Two of these are generally brown in color and the third is green. They look like tiny pieces of thread no more than a quarter of an inch long.

A hydra has a slender body that is shaped like a hot dog with a mouth at one end and a foot at the other. The foot is called a pedal disk, and it is slightly wider than the animal's body. This pedal disk can be used by the hydra to cling to the surface of a submerged leaf or pebble on the pond floor or to move the animal about. The hydra's mouth is surrounded by five or six tentacles.

If you see hydras on a water weed from a pond, place the weed in a white bowl filled with clean pond water—not tap water, which often has chemicals in it that can harm these animals—and leave it for a few hours. The animals will leave the leaf and slowly move to the side of the bowl, attracted by the lighter color.

A hydra budding

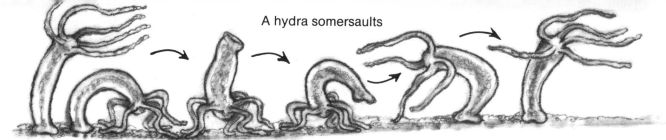

A hydra somersaults

Although a hydra can glide over a surface on its pedal disk, it also can float by attaching the disk to a bubble of air or it can walk along the ground by performing submerged somersaults. To do this, it anchors the disk, then bends its mouth and tentacles to the ground. Then it throws the pedal disk end over its head and reanchors it.

If hydras are put into a healthy aquarium, they can live for a long time, eating the various one-celled animals in the water.

A hydra's body is very flexible, like Silly Putty. When the animal has been disturbed or annoyed, it contracts into a round ball. But when it is calm again, it takes its hot-dog shape. Then the tentacles can often reach an inch in length.

Since the hydras cannot see, they must rely completely on touch and taste to gather food. The waving tentacles increase their chances of bumping into something or something bumping into them. When a one-celled animal or a larger pond inhabitant, like a water flea, touches any of the tentacles, the stinging cells are triggered and shoot out. Some of them deliver poison and others wrap themselves around the food. Slowly the tentacles close and draw the victim into the hydra's mouth and on to the stomach. There have been known cases of a hydra's catching and holding a tiny fish.

Hydras can regrow lost parts. One hydra can be cut into several pieces and each piece will develop into a complete, new individual.

They reproduce by releasing eggs and sperm in the water. These meet to form *fertilized eggs* that eventually becomes a tiny new hydra. They can also reproduce from buds that form on their bodies. A tiny bump grows into a complete hydra, which then breaks off and starts a new life.

FLATWORMS

TAPEWORMS

PLATYHELMINTHES: Worms That Are Flat

Most of the animals that we have discussed up to now have been very small one-celled animals or groups of one-celled animals like sponges and the hydra. But the flatworms, of the phylum *Platyhelminthes* (pronounced pla′ti-hel-min′thez), are animals with bodies made of cells that work together to form one individual. These worms are flat like a ribbon, not round like earthworms. In the ancient Greek language, *Platy* is the word for flat and *helminth* means worm.

Most of the approximately fifteen thousand species of flatworms that have been identified by scientists are *parasites* on other animals, including cows, pigs, cats, dogs, and sometimes human beings.

A parasite is an animal that is dependent for food on another animal, called the *host.* This union of animals can last a long time or be a temporary thing. For example, when a mosquito bites your arm, the mosquito is the parasite and you are the host because you are providing blood for its food.

The tapeworm is one kind of flatworm that may be familiar to anyone who has ever had a dog or a cat. Tapeworms look like pleated white ribbon. The ribbon is divided into many individual pieces and often reaches a length of about two feet.

HOOKS

HEAD

At the front end of the ribbon is a very small, rounded knob with a mouth surrounded by tiny hooks, or suckers. Using these hooks, the tapeworm attaches itself to the inside of a dog's or cat's intestine. Here it gets all the food it needs. It is completely dependent on the host animal because it has no digestive system of its own.

Each one of the worm's segments is a whole animal, and when it breaks off and leaves the host's body, it is able to lay tiny eggs that fall on the ground. Sometimes a tapeworm egg can be eaten by a flea. The infected flea becomes a host to the egg and eventually the egg hatches to form a very tiny new tapeworm within the flea's stomach. If the infected flea is eaten by your pet, the tiny tapeworm then enters the body of your cat or dog.

Even though it sounds unpleasant, most parasites do not harm their hosts, but they can cause a dog or cat to lose weight and become very weak if it does not get enough food for itself *and* the tapeworm. There are drugs that will remove the tapeworm without harming its host.

A dog with a tapeworm

SEGMENTS

19

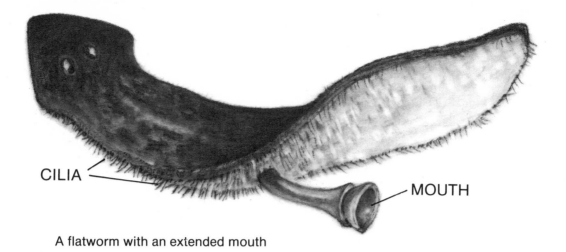

CILIA

MOUTH

A flatworm with an extended mouth

Another member of the phylum Platyhelminthes is the *planarian*. This flatworm is called free-living, because it does not act as a parasite on other animals. Most kinds of planarians have a mouth in the center of the front of their bodies, about the spot where your navel is. Usually the mouth is kept inside the body but when the planarian feeds, the mouth comes out just like the trunk of an elephant or a small vacuum cleaner. Planarians eat a large variety of living and dead food and can be fed tiny pieces of meat in the laboratory.

Planarian bodies are so flat that the animals seem to fit the shape of the rock or other surface upon which they glide. They seem to move without effort on a trail of slime produced by special cells on the front of the body. It is almost as if they row themselves from place to place on a river of slime with thousands of little oarlike *cilia* that cover their fronts. Each cilium is a hairlike part roughly the shape of one of your eyelashes.

There are two very common species of planarians that live in most freshwater ponds. Both kinds are often used in laboratory research because they are easy to keep.

If a planarian is cut into four pieces and the pieces are put back into clean pond water, each will soon grow into a complete individual. One planarian cut into four pieces will soon become four new ones.

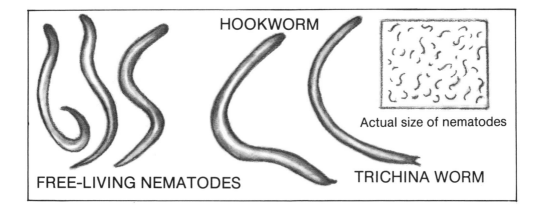

HOOKWORM

Actual size of nematodes

FREE-LIVING NEMATODES

TRICHINA WORM

NEMATODES: The Anywhere Animals

Wormlike animals called *nematodes* live almost everywhere on earth. They are in the phylum *Nemathelminthes* (pronounced nem-a-tel-min'thez). This word means threadlike in ancient Greek. Some biologists think there are over 500,000 different species of Nemathelminthes on the earth, but only 100,000 have been discovered and named. They are also called roundworms.

Nematodes are found in the tropical rain forests of Brazil and the pine forests of Canada; in streams and ponds; in mud and mud puddles; in the wet sand at the ocean's edge and in the dry dirt next to the front steps of your house. One spadeful of good garden soil usually contains about a million of them.

The largest of the nematodes is six feet long, but most of them are very small and can only be seen with a microscope or a good hand-held magnifying lens. Most of the dirt that you collect from a freshwater pond will contain some nematodes. Under a microscope, even at a low power, you will see these worms thrashing about in tiny particles of sand and soil.

Nematodes move through the thin film of moisture found in damp earth by pushing their bodies against particles of soil. However, in open water they are very poor swimmers.

Most nematodes are *carnivores*, or meat eaters. They eat

microscopic animals, including protozoans, and also decaying plant material. Some are parasites of living plants. The foods of these animals are called *microorganisms*, a group of plants and animals that include the one-celled protozoa. When times are hard, nematodes will eat a piece of mold, but they prefer a plump and juicy amoeba or paramecium.

A nematode caught in the sticky strands of an underground fungus

Nematodes have no eyes or ears. They sense vibrations through the touch of long and short tentacles that grow about their mouths. Two spots on top of their heads are not eyes, but more like noses. They are used to smell out food and enemies. Some nematodes have big teeth and fangs and others have a mouth for sucking, much like a soda straw.

Nematodes have few internal organs. They are basically eating machines. A nematode stomach and intestine is one simple sac that both digests and then absorbs the food. Unlike a human stomach, which fits neatly inside and just above the navel, the nematode's digestive system runs straight through, almost from its mouth to the tip of its tail.

A few nematodes live in the intestines of warm-blooded animals like cows, horses, and humans. They are parasites that depend on the host animal for their food.

One of the most harmful of these parasites is called a *trichina* (trik-i'na) worm. It can live in the stomach and muscle of pigs and some other mammals and even cause death by destroying these muscles. The animals can get infected from eating raw garbage that contains meat infested with young nematodes. A human can get the parasite from eating pork that is undercooked. The heat of thorough cooking will kill the parasites.

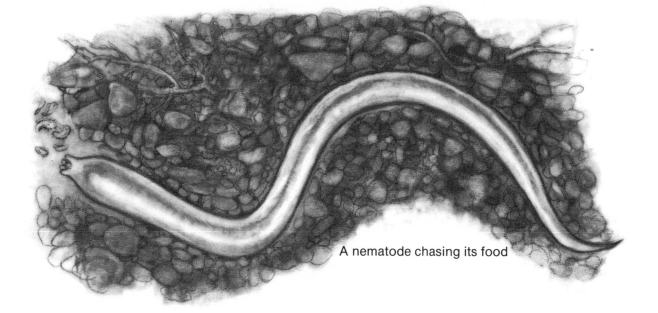

A nematode chasing its food

The harmful worms are only a small part of this large animal family. Most roundworms do not cause injury or disease. But by eating bacteria, Protozoa, tiny plants, and parts of dead animals, they eventually turn this food into natural chemical compounds and help make fertile soil.

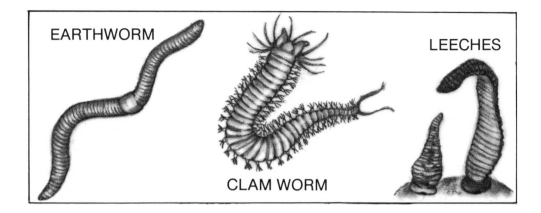

EARTHWORM

CLAM WORM

LEECHES

ANNELIDA: Everyday Earthworms

The earthworm is a very common animal. Most people who fish have used earthworms as bait, and gardeners know that when worms are found in the soil, it usually means the soil is in good condition. The earthworm is the first animal that we have looked at that can be said to have a "brain." The word *brain* is in quotation marks because the earthworm does not have a real brain as complicated as a human one, but it has a concentration of nerve endings in its front end that controls its activities.

Earthworms are called segmented worms because their bodies are arranged in rings or segments. They belong to the phylum *Annelida* (An-ne-li′da), a word that comes from the French language and means to arrange in rings. The phylum contains about ten thousand species, which are found in oceans, fresh water, and moist soil.

The typical earthworm is divided into 100 to 180 rings. Each ring is easy to see, and by counting them, you can locate the inner organs of the worm. The brain, for example is found in ring number three, and the worm's five pairs of hearts are in rings seven through nine.

Animals with backbones have only one heart, but the

earthworm needs ten in order to provide the pressure needed to pump blood from one end of it to the other. The large blood vessels nearest the hearts branch out to become many smaller tubes that carry food and oxygen in the blood to all parts of the animal's body. Earthworm blood has a chemical in it that makes its blood red in color. This red chemical helps the earthworm to take in oxygen for breathing.

The swelling found on rings thirty-one through thirty-seven produces a sort of cocoon that holds the earthworm's eggs. This cocoon is buried in the soil where the eggs hatch into tiny worms.

Earthworms do not have any eyes, so they can't see to find food. They plow ahead entirely by feel. If the front knob on the worm's body comes in contact with food, the food is pushed into the worm's open mouth at the bottom of ring number one. There, an organ that acts like a suction pump pulls the food toward the stomach.

An earthworm also has a *gizzard*, which is located in rings seventeen and eighteen. This is a very muscular pouch that is lined with an extremely hard material called *chitin*, the same material found in the shells of clams and lobsters and in insect bodies. The gizzard acts like a food processor, grinding up the minerals, dirt particles, bits of leaf, and anything else that the

MOUTH

BRAIN

1
3

7 8 9

17 18

HEARTS

GIZZARD

worm takes in its mouth. The intestine runs from ring nineteen to the end of the worm, where food wastes exit in neat little piles called worm castings.

Earthworms move by expanding and contracting. On both sides of each ring, there is a pair of hooks. When the worm wants to move ahead, it holds onto the ground with the hooks at its back end, loosens the ones in the middle and front, and pushes its way forward with its very powerful muscles. Then it drops hooks at the front, releases the rest of the hooks, and pulls up the rear.

One hundred and fifty years ago, the scientist Charles Darwin wrote a famous book about earthworms. He found that soil that contained them was far better for plants than soil without them. As the worms tunnel through the dirt, they actually break down small bits of valuable minerals into even smaller pieces and, at the same time, mix bits of soil and organic matter together. This in turn is made even smaller by the actions of roundworms like nematodes, and eventually it all becomes a nutritious "soup" that the roots of plants can easily absorb.

Fresh air enters the soil through earthworm tunnels and brings oxygen deep down where it is used by the living things in the soil. At the same time, the tunnels improve the drainage of water through the ground. Earthworms can also burrow deep into the earth and bring fresh soil to the surface.

WORM CASTINGS

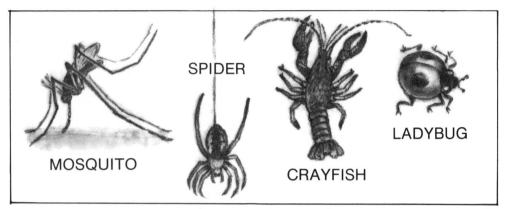

SPIDER

MOSQUITO

LADYBUG

CRAYFISH

ARTHROPODA: Animals with Outside Skeletons

More animals belong to the phylum *Arthropoda* (pronounced arth-ro-po'da) than any other. There are almost 800,000 species in this phylum, and counting the animals yet to be discovered, there may be well over one million.

Arthropods include crawling centipedes and millipedes, with their many legs; spiders; beetles, houseflies, grasshoppers, and other insects; shrimps, crabs, and lobsters.

Unlike the human body, which has skin-covered muscles that are attached to an inside skeleton, the arthropods have skin that is almost as hard as armor to protect soft insides. The skin is made of a number of hard materials in layers, so that it is very strong. This special skin is called an *exoskeleton* (*exo* is a Greek word meaning outside). An animal covered with an exoskeleton can still move easily because its legs have special protected joints, just like those in a suit of armor. *Arthro* is a Greek word for jointed, and *poda* means foot.

Some arthropods have very heavy and hard exoskeletons, such as crabs and lobsters, while others, like flies, mosquitoes, and other insects, have lighter exoskeletons. But all these exoskeletons are strong enough to protect the animals' fragile insides.

HOUSE SPIDER

WOLF SPIDER

One kind of arthropod is the spider. Insects have six legs and wings; spiders have eight legs and are always wingless. Spiders do not have true jaws, so they can't chew. Instead, they eat by spitting out digestive juices that turn the body of the prey into a liquid that they then eat by sucking, like soda through a straw.

Spiders have eyes—just like tiny versions of human eyes— except that spiders have eight of them, rather than two.

Some insects also have organs that produce silk, but spiders have the most complicated ones known. With these organs, called *spinnerets*, they spin egg sacs to protect their eggs; make draglines that can be used as ropes, swings, or parachutes; spin large and complicated webs that are like sticky nets for capturing other animals for food; and construct the very strong lines needed to hold up the webs. The spider waits at the edge of the web net for its prey to be caught in it, then wraps this meal in silk until it's time to eat.

On warm and golden days in late spring or early fall, when skies are crisp and blue, newly hatched baby spiders, called *spiderlings*, take wing on fresh breezes to see the world.

Leaving the protection of its cocoon, an almost weightless spiderling climbs up to the top of a branch or blade of grass.

SPIDERLINGS

There it points its tail end to the sky and shoots out a line often hundreds of times its own length. Soon, this line is caught by the wind and the spiderling flies away on it.

Harvestmen, or daddy longlegs, are not really spiders. They have only two eyes and no spinning glands at all. Still, they are close relatives, and because of their eight legs, they are often mistaken for true spiders.

Daddy longlegs sometimes kill tiny insects for food, but they usually feed on sap and the juices of overripe fruits.

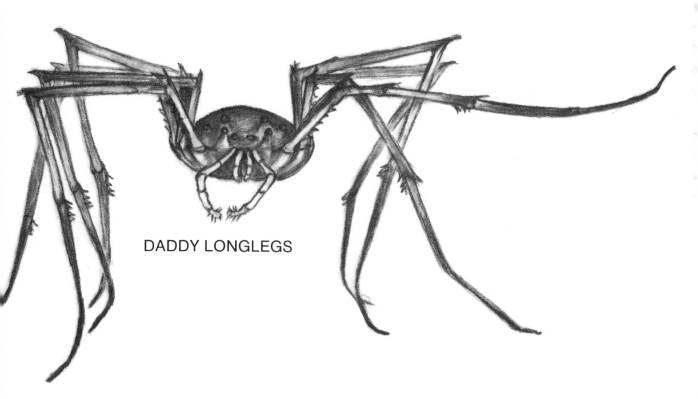

DADDY LONGLEGS

ARTHROPODA: Four Different Insects

Insects are probably the most successful group of animals on the earth. Humankind, with all the might of science at its command, is often brought to a complete halt by these animals. Some insects, like Japanese beetles, aphids, and grasshoppers, can do terrible damage to food crops. But there are many other insects with fantastic shapes, brilliant colors, and lovely patterned wings that are harmless to people.

Like other arthropods, insects have exoskeletons, but unlike them, most insects have two pairs of wings and can fly.

There are some insects that cannot fly. One is the silverfish, a very small pest that lives in damp corners of houses and chews almost everything in sight. Another is the flea—a disease-carrying insect that has bothered fur-bearing animals and humans for centuries.

Honeybees are flying insects, and without their help in pollinating flowers, there would be no fruits: no apples, pears, or oranges. In their search for flower nectar, bees carry pollen from flower to flower, and this helps the flowers to produce seeds. Man

SUMMER MOSQUITO

has eaten the honey that bees make from nectar for over four thousand years.

There are many insects that are valuable to farmers in the fight against insect pests. A praying mantis, for example, can attack and eat insects that feed on grains and vegetables.

Silk cloth is made from the cocoon of the silkworm moth. The mosquito, the grasshopper, the butterfly, and the ladybug are all members of the insect family.

Mosquitoes are small insects with long legs. The female mosquito has a special mouth part that acts like a hypodermic needle. It can pierce skin and withdraw a small amount of blood, which the female needs to properly develop its eggs. The one good thing about the female mosquito is that she makes a warning whine with her wings as she prepares to land on a neck or an ear. Male mosquitoes do not sting. They feed on fruits and berries, and their wings don't whine.

In the warmer parts of the world, mosquitoes carry malaria, yellow fever, and other tropical diseases. In the cooler parts, they rarely carry disease but are still major pests because of their bites.

Grasshoppers "fiddle" by drawing one of their large hind legs across a membrane in their front wings. This makes that common sound heard on hot summer afternoons. The rattling sound that grasshoppers, also known as locusts, make when they jump is caused when they rap their wings together.

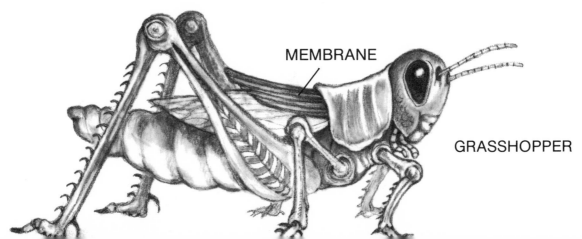

MEMBRANE

GRASSHOPPER

Grasshoppers have powerful jaws that are perfect for chewing vegetation. Most of the time, their chewing does little harm to crops, but sometimes they travel in huge swarms, and millions of grasshoppers, or locusts, may descend on fields of wheat and corn, eating every leaf in sight.

Butterflies are ugly ducklings. They begin life as caterpillars, eating their way from leaf to leaf. Then they literally turn into a tubular case called a *chrysalis* (pronounced kris′a-lis), usually found attached to a branch of a shrub or small tree.

After a month or two, the chrysalis splits open and a beautiful butterfly emerges. It dries its wings in the sun, then flies off in search of the nearest flower.

A butterfly has a special tongue, just underneath its eyes, that is shaped like a long, hollow tube. It is usually coiled like a watch spring, but it can be uncurled and used just like a flexible soda straw to suck the nectar from flowers.

RED ADMIRAL BUTTERFLY

Beetles are insects that have one pair of wings that have hardened into a shell-like case. They are usually large and make a great deal of noise when they fly. People often dislike beetles as a group.

But everybody likes ladybugs, or lady beetles, and they are among the most useful of insects as well as being members of the beetle clan. Ladybugs have enormous appetites—far out of proportion to their size—and will eat mealybugs, aphids, whiteflies, and scale, all plant pests. Even young ladybugs have tremendous appetites.

In California, ladybugs hibernate in huge masses. They can be collected in the fall and kept until the following spring to be released in orchards to attack mealybugs and aphids.

In the north, adult ladybugs spend the winter in loose window frames and cracks in wood. In late March, as the sun's rays become warmer, the little ladybugs wake up from their sleep and look for a meal.

LADYBUGS

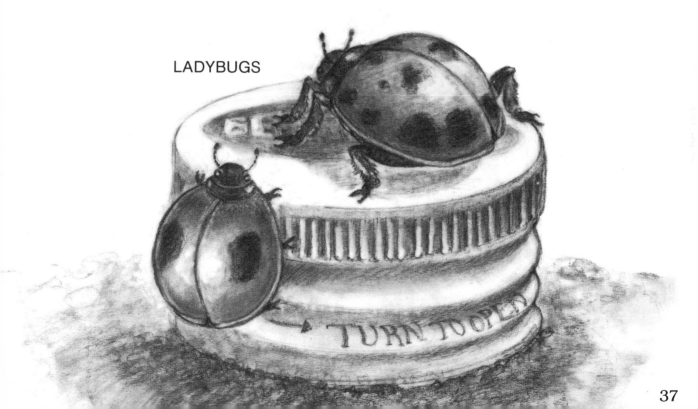

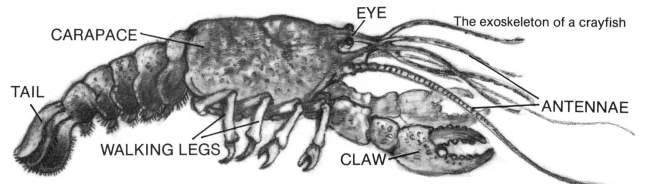

CARAPACE

EYE

The exoskeleton of a crayfish

TAIL

ANTENNAE

WALKING LEGS

CLAW

ARTHROPODA: Freshwater Lobsters

Crayfish, crawfish, or crawdad are all common names for an arthropod that looks like a lobster and lives in freshwater streams, along the edges of rivers, and in clean ponds. *Cray* and *craw* are old European words for crab. The fish ending was added because years ago, most animals from the water were called fish. Even today, we call scallops shellfish; the cuttlefish is really an octopus and the starfish is no fish at all.

Crayfish have five pairs of legs. The first pair is armed with claws that are used to grasp prey, although they are not strong enough to do any damage to a person's finger. Their exoskeleton shell is a bluish gray or brown, so they are almost invisible as they hide behind rocks to wait for small fish or insects to come along.

When a crayfish is surprised, it uses its strong tail to quickly push itself backward through the water.

Arthropods as a group are very successful animals. They have good eyes and a highly developed nervous system, and the exoskeleton provides excellent protection.

The one problem they have is growth. When a crayfish, for example, grows, its exoskeleton does not. The time eventually comes when the animal becomes too large for its shell. A larger, but soft, exoskeleton grows underneath the old one. Then the crayfish carefully hides itself while the old exoskeleton splits, for the soft, new shell can't protect it from its enemies. The new shell hardens in a day or two, and the animal goes back to a normal life.

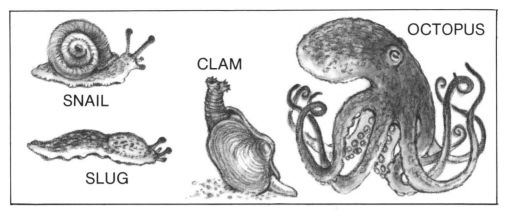

SNAIL

SLUG

CLAM

OCTOPUS

MOLLUSCA: Animals with Movable Homes

Most mollusks are marine animals that live in shells. They either carry their homes around with them on their backs, like snails, or lie buried in the ocean floor, like clams.

Snails live in coiled shells—often with beautiful shapes and brilliant colors—and many have trapdoors for additional protection. Clams and oysters live within a shell in the form of two halves or valves, held with an elastic hinge, which tightly clamp together. They are called *bivalves* (*bi* means two, and *valve* is from a Latin word for a folding door).

Octopuses and squid are also mollusks. They, too, have shells, but their shells are very small and hidden within their bodies. Finally, even the terrible garden slug is really a true snail, only its shell is so small as to be almost gone.

Some shells are so beautiful that people collect them. Until the invention of plastic, shirt and blouse buttons were all made from mother-of-pearl, the name of a shiny, hard material that lines the shells of clams and oysters.

A pearl is the only jewel produced by a living animal. Pearls are made by oysters and are the result of a grain of sand or other small object that itches and annoys the animal. To relieve the itch, the oyster covers the grain of sand with layers of mother-of-pearl.

Mollusks rank just behind arthropods in the great number of individual species, with more than 100,000 members. The name *mollusca* (pronounced mol-us′ka) is derived from the Latin word *mollis*, meaning soft.

Snails are mollusks that are members of the scientific family often called *gastropod*, from the Greek word *gastro*, meaning stomach, and *pod*, for foot, because they lack any legs or feet and literally walk on their stomachs. A snail's head usually bears two sets of small tentacles. The first set is basically for touch and feeling and the second pair has eyes at its tips.

Behind the head is the snail's mouth, but the major portion of its body outside the shell is its foot.

The snail uses a complicated system of muscles in the foot that both push and pull it. The foot is very strong, and it can hold tightly to a flat surface the same way that the suction cup on a play arrow will stick to glass.

Snails in the ocean breathe with gills. These are organs that resemble the grill on an air conditioner. The water passes through the gills, and small blood vessels in them take in oxygen. Slugs and land snails breathe through their lungs.

Slugs vary from one inch to six inches in length. Because they have no shell to protect their soft bodies from drying out in the open air, slugs must hide away from the heat of the sun,

A garden slug

spending the day hidden under rocks or pots in the garden. If you watch a slug in your garden at night, you can see it wave its touch tentacles, looking for something first to touch and then to eat.

A slug secretes a ribbon of silvery slime as it walks along. The slime trail can be seen shining on a leaf or rock long after the slug has gone.

A snail or slug has a tongue called a *radula*. This has rows of very hard teeth that tear apart plants (and sometimes other animals) and grind them into food.

Clams and other bivalves do not have radula since they filter their food from the ocean water through a set of sieves inside their bodies. Clams from polluted water can be very dangerous to eat. Their filtering systems can easily trap harmful bacteria in their bodies, and these bacteria can make people who eat them very ill.

A garden snail

A snail inside its shell

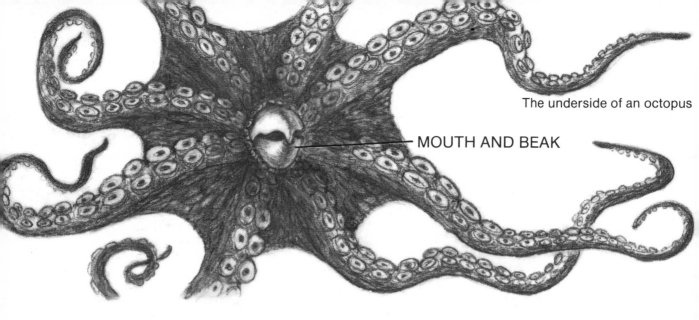

The underside of an octopus

MOUTH AND BEAK

Snails, slugs, clams, and oysters aren't very smart. But there are two other members of the mollusk family that are not only very fast but, compared to all the other animals that we have read about, very smart. They are the octopuses and the squids.

An octopus, for example, can be trained to avoid food presented on a plate that gives off a slight electric charge when touched by a tentacle. These animals can memorize various shapes both by sight and by touch and have been known to remember the information for several months.

Both octopuses and squid have very large eyes that are very close in structure to the human eye.

The foot found in most other mollusks has evolved in these animals into a set of tentacles, ten for the squid and eight for the octopus. These tentacles are covered with suckers that, once again, work like rubber suction cups.

Each squid and octopus has a radula in its mouth, but it also possess a pair of strong, horny beaks—very similar in looks to a parrot's beak—which are used in killing prey.

Each is also equipped with a special sac full of a dense black liquid that the animal can release to act like a smoke screen if it is frightened.

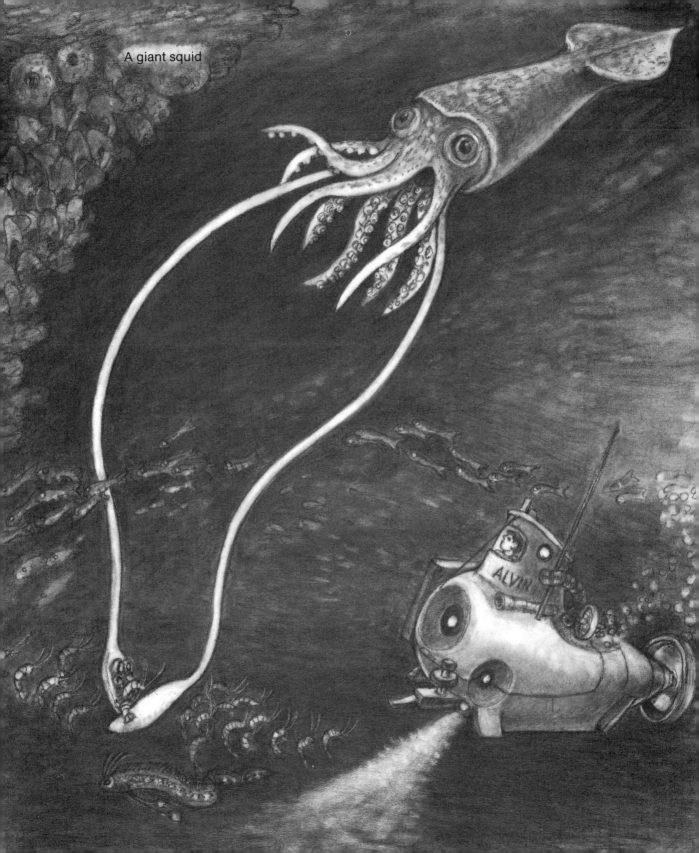
A giant squid

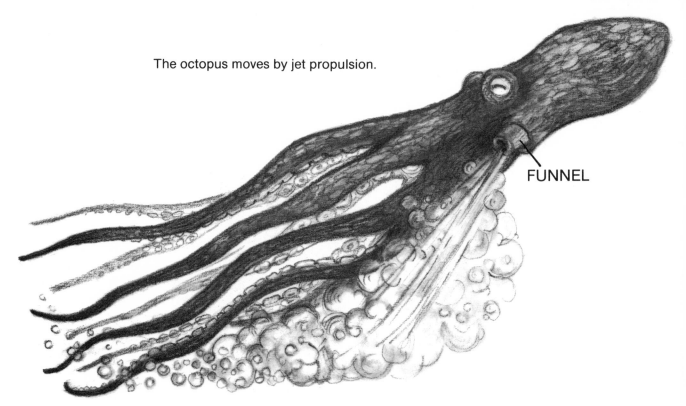

The octopus moves by jet propulsion.

FUNNEL

The most amazing thing about these animals is their method of transportation. Squid and octopuses have very thick, muscular bodies, each fitted with a movable funnel. They can fill their body cavities with water and aim the funnel opposite the direction they wish to go. By forcefully shooting the water out of the funnel, they move through the ocean by a kind of jet propulsion.

Giant squid, reaching more than fifty feet in length, exist in the deepest parts of the world's oceans. They are the largest invertebrates on earth.

In the year 1873, four Newfoundland fishermen were hauling in their herring nets and found that an easy job was turning into a struggle. When the edge of the net finally surfaced, the men were shocked to see that, instead of herring, they had caught a giant squid.

The next day, the squid was carefully measured. The body with the tentacles stretched out was over thirty-six feet long.

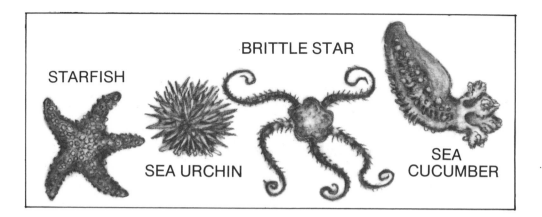

STARFISH

BRITTLE STAR

SEA URCHIN

SEA CUCUMBER

ECHINODERMATA: The Inside-Out Stomachs

Echinoderms live in the sea. Members of this last group of invertebrates belong to the phylum *Echinodermata* (pronounced e-ki'no-dur'ma-ta). *Echino* is the Latin word for hedgehog (a European animal like a porcupine), and *derma* is the word for skin. The word refers to the spines found on the skin of many of this phylum's members. All have five to twenty or more arms that radiate from a central disk. The most familiar member of this group is the starfish; the others include the sea urchin and sand dollar, sea cucumber, serpent star, and sea lily.

Echinoderms move about the ocean floor on hundreds of little tube feet. These feet are hollow and each is connected to a hollow ball set within the animal's body.

ube feet of starfish

In order to walk, the animal squeezes a number of the balls. The attached tube feet then fill up with water and stick out from openings in the arm, reaching the ocean floor. Each tube foot can move about like a little finger. By moving a number of "fingers" at the same time, the animal can travel along the ocean floor.

Starfish have another peculiar feature: an inside-out stomach. Biologists once believed the starfish pulled the two valves of a clam shell apart, using the combined strength of its arms and the suction of hundreds of the tube feet.

But now it is known that a starfish stands directly over the

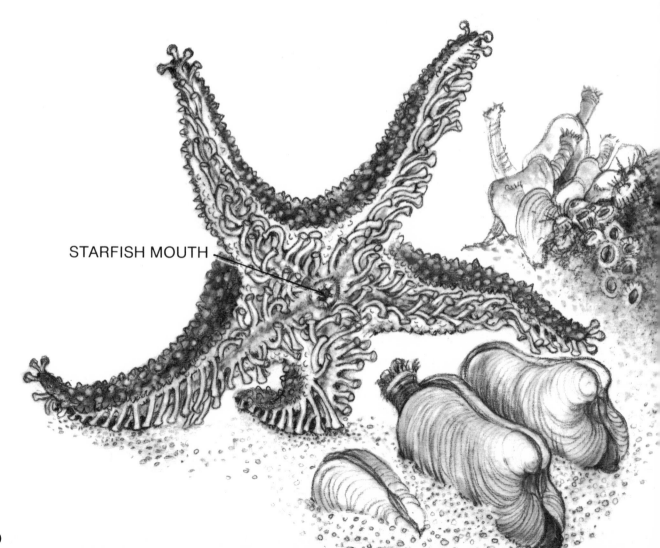

STARFISH MOUTH

clam and, using the force of the tube feet, pulls the calm shell apart—even a slight crack is enough—so tiny openings appear along the edge. Then the starfish drops its stomach sac to cover the clam and soon the starfish's digestive fluids pour through the tiny gaps to the clam's inside. Digestion begins and the clam weakens. Its muscles lose their strength, the shell opens a bit more, even more fluids enter, and the job is done.

Echinoderms have no hearts or kidneys or even brains. Unlike octopuses and squid, they will never learn from past mistakes. But many have such beautiful shapes and bright colors, they are always a pleasure to look at.

STARFISH STOMACH

GLOSSARY

Amoeba   A one-celled microscopic animal.

Amoebocyte   A cell in a sponge that moves around like an amoeba.

Annelida   The phylum that contains earthworms. It is a word that means to arrange in rings.

Arthropoda   The phylum that contains insects, spiders, and crabs. Most of these animals have very hard skins on the outside of their bodies.

Bivalve   An animal, such as a clam or oyster, with two shells hinged together.

Carnivore   An animal that eats meat.

Chitin   A very tough organic substance that forms part of the gizzard of an earthworm and the exoskeletons of arthropods.

Chrysalis   A tubular case that holds a caterpillar as it turns into a butterfly.

Cilia   A hairlike projection that looks like a human eyelash.

Cnidaria   The phylum that contains jellyfish, anemones, and hydras. The word means nettle. It refers to the stinging cells found on these animals, cells that resemble the stinging cells found in the nettle plant.

Craw and cray   The old European words used for crab.

Cytoplasm   A granular material found in animal cells.

Echinodermata   The phylum that contains starfish and sea urchins.

Exoskeleton   The name for a very hard skin found on the outside of many insects, crabs, and lobsters.

Fertilize   The union of a male cell, or sperm, and a female cell, or egg, which produces a new plant or animal.

Fossil   The remains of animals or plants that have turned to stone.

Gastropod   The scientific name for snails. It means stomach-footed.

Gizzard   A muscular pouch inside many animals, which is used to grind up food.

Host   An animal or plant that another animal or plant lives upon.

Invertebrate   An animal that does not have a backbone.

Microorganism   A tiny plant or animal that cannot be seen with the naked eye.

Microscope   A scientific instrument used to enlarge objects too small to be seen with the naked eye.

Mollusca   The phylum for clams and snails. Most of these animals live in shells.

Nematode   A wormlike animal that belongs in the phylum Nemathelminthes.

Nemathelminthes   The phylum that contains roundworms. The word means threadlike.

Nucleus   The part that controls many activities of the cell and also the animal's or plant's inherited traits.

Paramecium   A microscopic one-celled animal that looks like a tiny slipper.

Parasite   An animal that is dependent for food on another animal.

Pelvis   The bones at the lower part of a skeleton that the leg bones are attached to.

Phylum   A system of cataloging animals according to both their inside and outside physical appearance.

Planarian   A kind of flatworm that lives in freshwater ponds.

Platyhelminthes   The phylum for the flatworms.

Porifera   The word means full of holes and is the scientific name for the sponge phylum.

Protozoa   The word means first animal. Protozoans are microscopic one-celled animals, thought to be among the earliest inhabitants on earth.

Pseudopod   A fingerlike projection that amoebas form in order to move about and capture food.

Radula   The tongue of a snail or slug, which bears rows of hard teeth.

Silica   A very strong glasslike mineral often found in sponge spicules.

Sperm   The male reproductive cell.

Spicule   A piece of a tough material that helps to hold the softer parts of a sponge together.

Spiderling   A newly hatched baby spider.

Spinneret   The organ in a spider that produces the silky webs.

Spongin   A soft material used to hold the cells of a bath sponge together.

Trichina   A nematode parasite that a human can get from eating undercooked pork.

Vertebra   Any of the individual bones that form the backbone.

Vertebrate   An animal that has a backbone. Frogs, snakes, birds, and mammals are all vertebrates.

Volvox   A protozoan that is made of many one-celled animals living together in the shape of a ball.

Zoologist   A scientist who studies only animals. Botanists study plants. Biologists study the life processes of both plants and animals.

BIBLIOGRAPHY

Bayer, Frederick M., and Owre, Harding B. *The Free-Living Lower Invertebrates*. New York: Macmillan Publishing Company, 1968.
A survey of invertebrate biology concentrating on animal structure and including many illustrations.*

Coe, Wesley Roswell. *Starfishes, Serpent Stars, Sea Urchins and Sea Cucumbers of the Northeast*. New York: Dover Publications, Inc., 1972.
A reprint of a book originally published in 1912 but valuable for its descriptions of these animals.

Cook, Joseph J., and Wisner, William L. *The Phantom World of the Octopus and Squid*. New York: Dodd, Mead and Company, 1965.
A popular description of octopus and squid behavior.

Emerton, James H. *The Common Spiders of the United States*. New York: Dover Publications, Inc., 1961.
A reprint of a book originally published in 1902 but with a new key to common groups of spiders and a new bibliography.

Garnett, W. J. *Freshwater Microscopy*. London: Constable and Company, Ltd., 1965.
A book on using a microscope to explore the world of freshwater ponds.

Johnson, Willis H., Laugengayer, Richard A., DeLanney, Louis E., and Cole, Thomas A. *Biology*. New York: Holt, Rinehart and Winston, Inc., 1966.
A well-illustrated and concise book on general biology.

Lutz, Paul E. *Invertebrate Zoology*. Reading, Massachusetts: Addison-Wesley Publishing Company, 1986.
An up-to-date book on the latest views dealing with the biology of invertebrates.*

Morgan, Ann Haven. *Field Book of Ponds and Streams*. New York: G. P. Putnam's Sons, 1930.
Still the most perceptive and well-written book of the many field guides available on freshwater biology.

Russell-Hunter, W. D. *A Biology of Lower Invertebrates*. New York: Macmillan Publishing Company, 1968.
A modern survey with an emphasis on morphology, behavior, and selected aspects of evolution.*

———. *A Life of Invertebrates*. New York: Macmillan Publishing Company, 1979.
A well-written book dealing with the major invertebrate groups.*

Sherman, Irwin W., and Sherman, Vilia G. *The Invertebrates: Function and Form*. New York: Macmillan Publishing Company, 1970.
A laboratory survey of the invertebrates, with detailed experiments.*

Swain, Ralph B. *The Insect Guide*. New York: Doubleday and Company, Inc., 1952.
A well-illustrated and thorough survey of the insects of North America.

* *Illustrations are by the author of this book.*

INDEX

Boldface denotes illustration